THE VICTORIANS
RECONSTRUCTED

Liz Gogerly

Photographs by Martyn F. Chillmaid

WAYLAND

Other titles in this series:
The Home Front • The Romans
The Saxons and Vikings • The Tudors
For more information on this series and other Wayland titles, go to www.waylandbooks.co.uk

Conceived and produced for Wayland by

Nutshell
MEDIA

Intergen House, 65–67 Western Road, Hove BN3 2JQ, UK
www.nutshellmedialtd.co.uk

© Copyright 2003 Nutshell Media

Editor: Polly Goodman
Designer: Simon Borrough
All reconstructions set-up and photographed by: Martyn F. Chillmaid
Photograph page 27: Alvey & Towers

First published in Great Britain in 2003 by Hodder Wayland,
an imprint of Hodder Children's Books.

This paperback edition published in 2005
Reprinted in 2008 by Wayland

British Library Cataloguing in Publication Data
Gogerly, Liz
The Victorians. – (Reconstructed)
1. Great Britain – Social life and customs – 19th century – Pictorial works – Juvenile literature
2. Great Britain – History – Victoria, 1837–1901 – Pictorial works – Juvenile literature
I. Title
941'.081'0222

ISBN 978 0 7502 4770 2

Printed and bound in China

Wayland
338 Euston Road, London NW1 3BH

Wayland is a division of Hachette Children's Books,
an Hachette Livre UK Company, www.hachettelivre.co.uk

Cover photographs: main photo: two child miners push a wagon out of a pit; from top to bottom: a
Victorian street scene; a printer checks that a poster has printed properly; a boatman legs his narrowboat
through a tunnel; a butcher's shop; a chemist making pills.

Title page: A typical Victorian street scene.

Contents

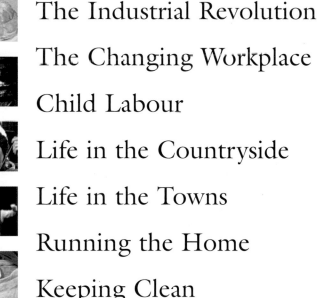

Who Were the Victorians?

A middle-class Victorian family dressed in their best clothes pose for a family portrait.

The Victorian era began in 1837 when Queen Victoria came to the throne. Victoria was just 18 years old when she became queen, and her reign would last until she died in 1901, aged 81. In 1840 Victoria married her German cousin, Albert, and over the next 17 years they had nine children together. The royal family was hugely popular and their happy family life became a role model for most families at the time. In 1861, the royal family was photographed together in one of the first ever portrait photographs. Soon after, many middle-class families had their photographs taken too.

Sailor suit

Satin and lace gown

Best hat

Lace frills

Cotton and lace shirt

Waistcoat, jacket and tie

By the mid-nineteenth century, there were millions of middle-class families living in Britain's industrial towns and cities. The father of each family had a respectable job such as a lawyer or banker. He worked hard to support his family, but in return he demanded obedience from his wife and children.

Most Victorian children knew the saying that 'children should be seen and not heard'. They had many rules to obey, such as keeping silent at the dinner table and not speaking unless they were spoken to. If they disobeyed, they risked being beaten with a leather strap.

In Victorian times there was no birth control, so many families had as many as ten children. Poorer families were usually crammed into small, overcrowded houses. Older children were expected to help their mothers run the home and look after their younger brothers and sisters. Children as young as 8 often had to work rather than go to school, to help provide for their family. It wasn't until 1870 that it became the law that all children aged between 5 and 13 had to go to school. Life for more wealthy children wasn't always easy either. They were usually raised by a nanny in the nursery and rarely saw their parents.

A girl with her *Girl's Own* annual, wearing clothes typical of the late nineteenth century.

Lace-up boots

Frilled dress

Girl's Own annual

Pinafore

High collar

Ringlets

The Industrial Revolution

A miner arrives at the pit early in the morning.

By the beginning of Queen Victoria's reign, Britain was known as 'the workshop of the world'. Large deposits of coal, iron, copper and tin provided the raw materials for industry, and Britain led the way in the industrial revolution. The country became the world's leading supplier of iron and steel, and its manufacturing industry was the envy of the world.

Coal was important to Britain's success because it was used to make steam, which powered factories and later, locomotives. Most industrial centres sprang up next to coalfields in northern England, Scotland and south Wales. Mining was back-breaking work, yet when demand for coal soared, children as young as 4 were often employed in the pits. Sometimes miners had to crawl along tunnels just 75 centimetres high. They faced hazards such as poison gas, and suffered bronchitis and asthma from the coal dust.

Miner

Site office

Coal

Pithead winding gear

In Victorian times, the only way of exporting or importing goods from abroad was by ship. At the end of the eighteenth century, the fastest way of transporting goods over long distances was on wooden sailing ships, called clippers. They carried tea and spices from Asia to England, and manufactured goods to North America.

At the beginning of the nineteenth century, new technology was transforming the shipbuilding industry and the first steamships started to replace sailing ships. These ships needed a lot of coal on board and had to make stops to refuel. The race was on to design ships that would be strong enough to carry more coal, so they would not have to stop and refuel and the journeys would become shorter. Once more Britain led the way and in 1843 the engineer Isambard Kingdom Brunel designed and built the *Great Britain*, the first steamship made of iron.

Rope   Oakum

Barrel of tar   Wooden boat

Two boatyard workers roll oakum into rope. It will be knocked into the seams of wooden boats and covered in tar to make them watertight.

The Changing Workplace

During Victoria's reign, people flocked to the industrial towns and cities from the countryside in search of employment in factories, textile mills and mines. By 1881, it is estimated that over a third of Britain's working population was employed in manufacturing.

Apart from factory workers and miners, there was still a growing number of traditional craftsmen, such as carpenters, blacksmiths, shoemakers and tailors. Craftsmen like these had to complete seven-year apprenticeships before they became fully qualified.

Like everyone else in Victorian times, the craftsman's work was made easier by the new technologies that were being developed at the time. In the 1850s, a new type of sewing machine meant that shoemakers could work more quickly and make more shoes. From the 1870s, factory-made shoes also became available. The shoemaker was still kept in business though, making handmade shoes for his more well-off, or 'well-heeled' customers.

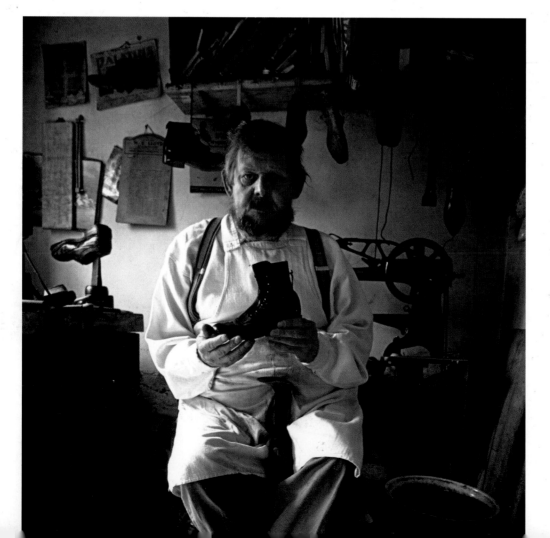

A shoemaker in his workshop.

Lace-up boot

Shoe last (mould)

Sewing machine

A printer checks that a poster has printed properly.

The Victorians invented machines for every kind of process imaginable. Some of these machines could be powered by steam, but many also relied on people. The first steam printing presses were being used in England in the early 1800s. The press was powered by steam, but the printer still had to select the individual wooden letters required.

Printer

Poster

Steam printing press

Wooden letter blocks

In the Victorian era, one new invention usually led to other exciting developments. For example in the nineteenth century, new advances in printing technology made it possible to print on both sides of a sheet of paper. Soon it was possible to print on rolls of paper rather than sheets. In turn, this meant that newspapers could be mass-produced and sold to many more people.

In 1851, Britain showed off its manufacturing achievements in the Great Exhibition, the world's first industrial fair. It was held in the Crystal Palace, a revolutionary building built out of glass and iron, in London.

Child Labour

Children were an important part of the Victorian workforce, but they were also the most badly treated. They provided cheap labour and because they were young, they were easy to boss about. In early Victorian times some children worked from five in the morning until nine o'clock at night. In the mines, children were employed to open doors or pick among the rubble to find pieces of coal. Children were also employed in factories. Their fast little fingers were perfect for working the machinery and their tiny bodies meant that they could crawl under moving machinery to clean it.

Two boys struggle with a wagon filled with coal.

Wagon

Coal

Cast-iron tracks

Pit entrance

Industrial towns attracted large numbers of single workers, which led to many unwanted children being born. These children were put in institutions such as workhouses, apprentice houses and hospitals for foundlings. Apprentice houses were run by owners of cotton mills and other factories. Children served apprenticeships in their factories for seven years, and in return they were fed, clothed, housed and schooled. Child apprentices would have known only discipline and hard work. Wardens supervised their every move and when they weren't working in the factory, they had lessons or tended the garden and mended clothes. Even so, they would have counted themselves lucky not to be in the workhouse.

Social campaigners like Anthony Ashley, the 7th Earl of Shaftesbury, fought to change the laws regarding child labour. In 1833, the first of a series of new laws meant that children under the age of nine were not to be employed in factories. Later, this age limit was raised and the working day was cut to ten hours. However, the new laws didn't help the thousands of children who worked in illegal sweat shops, or slaved on farms. In the 1870s, it became law for all children aged between 5 and 13 to go to school, but poverty and family hardship meant many children carried on working after school hours.

The dormitory of this apprentice house would have seemed luxurious compared to the workhouse.

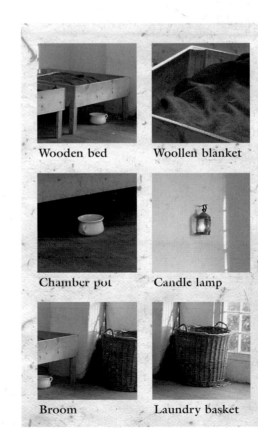

Wooden bed | Woollen blanket

Chamber pot | Candle lamp

Broom | Laundry basket

Life in the Countryside

A woman feeds her pigs with kitchen waste to fatten them up before killing them.

Sty

Bucket of feed

Vegetable patch

Squatters' cottage

For those families left in the Victorian countryside, life was tough. In the late eighteenth and early nineteenth century, rich landowners had taken over common land to use for commercial farming. People who had worked on the land for centuries suddenly had to rent the land off landowners, or work as labourers on their farms. The industrial revolution brought more hardship to farm labourers because steam-powered machinery replaced many of their jobs. Cheap imports of grain from America meant that many farmers turned to livestock farming instead. Farm labourers had to survive on smaller and smaller wages.

Poor families living in the countryside relied on animals and vegetables which they raised and grew themselves. Some families kept a cow for milk and cheese, raised chickens for eggs, and pigs for meat. When it was slaughtered, just before the winter, every part of the pig would have been eaten. The tongue would have been pickled, the ears and trotters used to flavour stews and soups, and the fat would have been spread on bread.

Many cottages were built on common land to avoid paying rent to a landowner. These were called squatters' cottages, and they often consisted of two small rooms, where families of seven or eight would live. The family would have gathered wood for fuel and made their own furniture. Clothes were handed down from one generation to the next. In the wintertime, the family would have gone to bed early so they didn't burn too many candles.

In the kitchen of a squatters' cottage, a woman checks the stew cooking on the range.

Bedroom

Stew pot

Hessian apron

Colander

Firewood

Iron

Life in the Towns

Families that moved to industrial towns had mixed fortunes. Factory workers found they had money in their pockets, but they worked long hours to earn it. Often they lived in overcrowded streets in houses that had been built quickly on the doorsteps of factories. In Leeds, Manchester and other industrial cities, large families crammed into back-to-back houses with no toilets or running water. In cities like Glasgow, families lived in single rooms in large tenement blocks. Wherever working-class people lived, the air hung with smoke that billowed out of the factories. Children had nowhere to play except the dirty streets, which were filled with slops and piles of horse dung.

By 7 a.m. in a Victorian street, people have already started their working day.

Laundry woman

Pub landlord

Milk-delivery boy

Slops

In a townhouse kitchen, a woman puts a kettle on the range.

Inside a typical working-class family's townhouse, the cast-iron range was at the heart of the home. Its hot surfaces heated water for food and washing, and it had an oven in the centre. Stews and soups were often put in the oven in the morning so they would be ready at night. As dinner bubbled away in the oven, the washing was usually hung up to dry over the range. At night, families gathered in the kitchen to warm themselves around the dying embers. Some families couldn't afford a range, so they took their meals to a communal oven, or to the baker's to be cooked, instead.

Later in the nineteenth century, conditions in towns began to improve. Gas lighting was introduced, and shops, hospitals, churches, schools, public houses and music halls sprang up. Towns became places where people could better themselves. The educated or ambitious could take respectable, white-collar jobs in banking, insurance or education. They became the middle classes, and they looked for homes to reflect their new status. Hundreds of houses were built away from the industrial smog, on the outskirts of towns. Families living in the suburbs had bigger homes with gardens.

Range

Kettle

Washing

Bread

Iron and stand

Hot-water bottle

Clothes pegs

Frying pan

Keeping Clean

In Victorian times, people were not as clean as we are today. In the early nineteenth century, most people washed their hands, face and feet every day, and had a bath every Saturday, when the whole family would share the water. Homes that could afford running water were only supplied for a few hours a day. Everybody else had to collect water from taps and wells in the street. If they wanted hot water, they had to boil it on the range.

Later in the nineteenth century metal pipes were introduced, which connected more homes to the water supply. By the 1890s, most middle-class homes had bathrooms with hot running water and daily bathing became fashionable. A wide variety of toiletries became available and advertisements for sweet-smelling soaps and perfumed talcum powders regularly appeared in ladies' magazines.

A man carefully shaves himself with a cut-throat razor.

Jug of water

China basin

Soap

Shaving jug

Shaving brush

Using a cut-throat razor

Tippler toilet

Newspaper

Most people only used
the outside toilet in the
daytime. At night, it
was usually too cold
and dark, so they used
chamber pots instead.
Torn-up newspaper was
used for toilet paper.

Sewerage was one of the biggest problems in Victorian towns.
The open sewers not only smelt bad, they caused terrible diseases
such as typhoid and cholera, which struck whole communities.
Most working-class people had outdoor toilets, often shared
with a whole row of houses. Tippler toilets had to be 'flushed
out' with a bucket of water after being used. At night people
used chamber pots, which they emptied each morning into
open sewers, called cesspools. The cesspools had to be emptied
regularly by 'night soil men'. In 1858, the Thames was so full
of waste that an appalling stink rose up from the river and forced
parliament to close.

By the middle of the nineteenth century, reformers had begun to
look for ways of dealing with the sewage problem. In 1848, the
Public Health Act stated that all new homes should have a toilet.
The changes were slow, but in the following decades new types
of flushing toilets were invented, and most cities established an
underground network of sewers.

Activities

pp4–5 Who Were the Victorians?

- Ask your parents if there are any old family photographs from Victorian times, or look for photographs of Victorian families in books. Compare them with photographs of your family today.
- Write a letter to a Victorian child, asking them what you'd like to know about their everyday life. Describe the things you can do in the twenty-first century that they could not do in the nineteenth century. Ask a member of your class to write back as if they were the Victorian child.

pp6–7 The Industrial Revolution

- Write a newspaper report about a terrible coal-mining disaster. If you live in an old coal-mining region, look at newspapers in your local library to find out about accidents that happened in your area.
- Look at the census for your area in your local library. Find a census for between 1841 and 1891. What was the main occupation in your area? How has it changed today?

pp8–9 The Changing Workplace

- Interview your local shoe-repairer to find out what has changed since being a shoemaker in Victorian times. Compare the equipment he or she uses today with the equipment in the photo on page 8.
- Design a poster for the print shop on page 9 to make. It could be an advertisement for a job, or for goods.

pp10–11 Child Labour

- Imagine what it was like for a poor child working in a coal mine. Write a diary entry about a typical day, starting when you got out of bed.

- Write a short play about a group of child apprentices who are planning to run away from their apprentice house.

pp12–13 Life in the Countryside

- Write a timetable for a day in the life of a squatter family. Include jobs such as feeding the pigs, gathering firewood, tending the vegetable patch, cooking and cleaning.
- Draw a plan of the house on page 13. Label the position of the range, beds for six children and two adults, a table and chairs.

pp14–15 Life in the Towns

- Compare the street where you live with the street in the photo. Look at the buildings, the pavement and the jobs people are doing. What are the similarities and differences from your street?
- Look at the housing in your area and find out when it was built. Was it built for working-class or middle-class people? If you live in a Victorian house, think about how it has changed since it was built.

pp16–17 Running the Home

- Write a diary for a day in the life of a working-class Victorian housewife. Include jobs such as throwing out the slops, washing and mending clothes.
- Imagine you are the wealthy owner of a Victorian house. Write a list of instructions for your maid telling her the jobs she needs to do in the next week.

pp18–19 Keeping Clean

- Hunt through old Victorian magazines for advertisements for toiletries. Design your own advertisement for a new product.
- Write a newspaper report with a shocking headline about the 'Great Stink' in London in 1858.

Celtic villages

The Celts lived in small villages in the countryside. Th[ey] were a farming people, and most families owned a nu[mber] of sheep, cattle and other animals. As Boudicca was b[orn] into a rich family, they would have owned many anim[als.] They would probably have had a large **roundhouse** wh[ere] they lived, ate and slept. They probably also had sever[al] other smaller thatched buildings which were used for keeping animals and storing food.

▲ This copy of a Celtic roundhouse has been built at Little Bu[tser,] Hampshire. The walls and roof were made of small tree trunk[s. The] walls were filled in with wattle and daub (mud and sticks), an[d the] roof was thatched with grasses.

The Celts

For 800 years, the Celts were the most powerful people [in] Europe. From about 800 BC, their **civilization** spread o[ver] most of mainland Europe and the British Isles. The Cel[tic] tribes never united to form a single nation, and differe[nt] languages were always spoken from tribe to tribe. The [Celts] were warlike people.

pp20–21 Food Shopping

- Write a shopping list for a poor family of ten in about 1900. Remember you don't have a fridge, so don't buy anything that won't keep. Include the shops you will visit for each type of food.
- What kind of shops are in your local area? Were any of them built in Victorian times? How have they changed since that time?

pp22–23 Disease and Medicine

- Visit your local library and use the microfilm to look at local newspapers from Victorian times. Look at the advertisements for health products and medicines. Make up your own advertisement for a new kind of health product.
- Ask your local chemist how pills are made today. Compare it with the way the chemist is making pills in the photo on page 23.

pp24–25 Getting Around

- Imagine you are a time-traveller who has been transported back in time to a Victorian town for a day. Write a tourist guide about the sights and sounds of the city.
- Look at maps of your local area and find out if any canals were built near you. Are they still in existence? Do people still use them today?

pp26–27 The Railway Age

- Design a poster for a Victorian railway station advertising day trips or holidays at the seaside.
- Write a story about a school day trip to the seaside in Victorian times. Discuss things like what the railway station was like, what it felt like to be on board a train and how fast the train went.

Finding Out More

Books to Read

All About the Industrial Revolution by Peter Hepplewhite and Mairi Campbell (Hodder Wayland, 2002)

All About the Victorians by Jane Goodwin (Hodder Wayland, 2001)

Digital Time Traveller: The Real Victorians (TAG Publishing, 2003)

The Illustrated World of The Victorians by Richard Wood and Sara Wood (Hodder Wayland, 2001)

In Their Own Words: The Victorians by Robert Hull (Watts, 2003)

The Past in Pictures: The Victorians by John Malam (Hodder Wayland, 2002)

Who? What? When?: Victorians by Bob Fowke (Hodder Children's Books, 2003)

Places to Visit

The Boat Museum, South Pier Road, Ellesmere Port, Cheshire CH65 4FW
The photograph of the man legging through a tunnel was taken at this museum, which houses boats and equipment used in Victorian times.

The Black Country Living Museum, Tipton Road, Dudley, West Midlands DY1 4SQ
Many of the photographs that appear in this book, including the street scenes, the chemist's shop and the Victorian kitchen were taken at this museum.

Blists Hill Victorian Town, Legges Way, Madeley, Telford, Shropshire TF7 5DU
The squatter's cottage, the cobbler's shop and the butcher's shop are all part of this recreation of a late-Victorian working town.

Boudicca's early

Although Boudicca is famous, very little is k[nown] about her early life. All we know is that s[he was] born about the year AD 30 and that her family w[ere] probably important **aristocrats** who lived in the re[gion] now known as East Anglia. Boudicca is sometimes know[n by] her Roman name of Boadicea, and she was probably nam[ed after] the **Celtic** goddess of Victory, Boudiga.

Leaving home

Like the children of most Celtic families, Boudicca would [have] been sent away as a young girl to join the **household** of [an] aristocratic family. There she would have received her edu[cation,] learning about the history and **customs** of her **tribe**. This exchange of children was an important way of building friendships and loyalty between different families and trib[es.]

While she was g[rowing] up, Boudicca [was] also trained [as a] **warrior**. Th[ere was] special train[ing] where girls a[nd boys] were taught h[ow to fight] with swords an[d to] ride horses and [drive] **chariots**.

◀ The Celts w[ere fine] artists and the[ir] metalwork wa[s prized] throughout Eu[rope. This] **bronze** cow's [head was] probably the h[andle on a] ceremonial buc[ket.]

The royal inheritance

King Prasutagus had been ruler of the Iceni for at least five years when he married Boudicca. **Celtic** kings did not always **inherit** their position from their fathers. They were often **elected** by the other noble men in the **tribe**, or became king by marrying the queen.

An unsuccessful rebellion

In about AD 49 or 50, a number of tribes in south-eastern England rose up against the Roman armies that had invaded England in AD 43. The **rebellion** was quickly crushed by the Romans. King Prasutagus had been one of the leaders of the rebellion, but he was allowed to keep his lands and his throne. However, the Romans now recognized him as a **client-king**, only accepted for as long as he did as he was told by them.

The death of Prasutagus

In about AD 61, King Prasutagus died. Boudicca was now about thirty years old and her two daughters were about eleven and twelve. Boudicca became **regent** of the Iceni, that is she became their ruler until a new king could be chosen by the tribal chiefs.

◀ This Roman coin shows the head of Nero, who was emperor at the time of Boudicca's rebellion. It was made in AD 55. The head behind Nero is his mother, Agrippina.

The king's will

Prasutagus had left a **will** when he died. This gave half his property and lands to the Roman **emperor**. As a client-king, who was under the control of the Romans, this was expected. He left the other half of his property to Boudicca and their two daughters. Prasutagus probably believed that he had left a peaceful settlement behind him, satisfying both the Romans and his family. Events were quickly to prove how wrong he was.

▶ Claudius was emperor at the time of the Roman invasion of Britain. This **bronze** head of Claudius was found in the River Alde in Suffolk.

The Roman conquest of Britain

In AD 43 the Roman emperor Claudius launched an invasion of Britain. Many of the British tribes, especially in southern England, surrendered to the invading army. Others continued to fight the Romans fiercely. It was to be many years before all the southern tribes were defeated. The Romans never succeeded in conquering Scotland.

Index